THE QUIET CUPID

An Introvert's Guide to Winning in

Love, Relationships, and Marriage

Tim L. Gardner

TABLE OF CONTENTS

INTRODUCTION

T hank you for obtaining your personal copy of *The Quiet Cupid: An Introvert's Guide to Winning in Love, Relationships, and Marriage.* Congratulations on doing so.

The following chapters will discuss some of the many components of an introverted personality and how those traits and tendencies might affect an introvert's love life. They also go into great detail about how to succeed in love as an introvert. Chapter 1 covers some defining characteristics and common challenges that introverts experience. Chapter 2 examines the dating stage and how to navigate it as an introvert. In chapter 3, readers will learn strategies for developing and managing relationships as an introvert.

You will discover how important understanding and coming to terms with your introverted personality truly is. Understanding oneself will help an individual succeed in love, dating, and marriage. When you have a solid grasp on your personality, you can build on your strengths and identify potential changes to be made.

The final chapter will explore marriage, a huge step in the progression of romantic relationships. Introverts will benefit from navigating marriage differently than their non-introverted peers. In addition, marrying a fellow introvert has the potential to develop into of the most rewarding experiences in this world.

The internet and digital publications market are filled with books, websites, and courses on this topic. However, many of them are targeted at general audiences, thus failing to accommodate for introverted personality types and their unique circumstances. This book seeks to help introverts develop the tools that will bring them success in the world of romantic relationships, including dating and marriage.

CHAPTER 1

SO, YOU'RE AN INTROVERT.

Introverts are known to exude a number of characteristics that often complicate their love lives. That is not to say, however, that introverts have more adversity when it comes to romantic relationships. Rather, like other personality types, introverts are faced with their own unique challenges in the realms of love, relationships, and marriage. Those challenges, which will be explored a little later on in this book, often lead to miscommunications, misunderstandings, and disagreements, all of which can, in turn, lead to arguments and escalations of the conflict.

If you have ever found yourself caught in a relationship in which you felt like your partner was unaccommodating of your specific needs, then you will want to read this book through to the end. Perhaps you just wanted to spend time in the presence and proximity of your partner while each of you just did your own thing, only to have your companion accuse you of being distant and quiet.

Or, maybe you are a more reflective, contemplative introvert. You might like to go into great depth of thought, considering how other people interpret your actions. This can cause anyone to spend obscene amounts of time crafting the perfect text replies, obsessing over the perfect words to type out to their partner. As a result, your partner feels neglected when you fail to reply to them in a timely manner, if at all. This book will show you how to manage your introverted tendencies in such a way that has a positive impact on your love life.

You might also experience the social fatigue that comes along with an introverted personality. For example, you might feel wholly unprepared to interact with people just moments before your first date, simultaneously not wanting to cancel or no-show. This predicament can lead to small anxiety attacks while the introverted person begins to frantically contemplate rescheduling.

Other introverts report enjoying a long-distance relationship, but having serious reservations about spending time with their romantic interest in person because they fear that their quiet personality will come off as standoffish. More introverts still complain about family members making intrusive inquiries as to why they do not spend more time with their long-distance partners.

Some people with introverted personalities have had an otherwise wonderful date take a turn for the worse as soon as the interaction moved to a crowded, loud venue. Such places have the potential to wipe out the energy levels of even the most resilient introverts.

A number of introverts also struggle with getting labeled as "quiet." A number of introverted tendencies can cause an individual to behave in a reserved fashion, but when a peer group assigns a label to one of their own, that label reinforces the behavior that it refers to. For example, after enough people nonchalantly told me, in one way or another, that I am "quiet," I started to realize that I was, in fact, very quiet. I even recall saying to myself after one such conversation, in an accepting tone, "Oh yeah, I guess I am quiet." If enough people tell you that you are quiet, you will start to become more and more quiet as you step into the role that your peer group has assigned to you. The challenge, then, comes about when you have to navigate your own dating life while simultaneously managing the social expectations that your peer group has of you. The contents of this publication seek to help introverted individuals overcome the unique challenges that they face. The love, relationships, and marriage portions of introverts' lives will undergo new perspectives. The manageable methods described in this book will provide insight and tips that give introverts the power to enjoy a dating life that effectively navigates the specific challenges that introverts face.

Challenges That Introverts Face

The unique personality traits of most introverts present them with a series of challenges in the way of romantic relationships. Introverts often know that they exist in this world behaving and thinking in ways that might not make sense to the rest of the population. However, introverts understand one another and recognize the reasoning behind some of their identifiable personality traits, including their own gentle natures, thoughtfulness, desires for privacy, high sensitivity levels, and mysteriousness.

First, introverts have to contend with the fact that they are, in general, more gentle than their extroverted counterparts. In most cases, the willingness and ability to behave in a gentle manner are virtuous. However, when it comes to dating, adopting an overly gentle nature will make it difficult to meet new potential partners. Consider a single adult man who is out at a nightclub, looking to meet his next girlfriend. This man has to contend with the other single men in his proximity as they compete for attention from the attractive females in the venue. As such, the men in the room must take it upon themselves to stand out in such a way that attracts female attention. A man who goes through this kind of situation with an insistence on maintaining a gentle disposition will get lost amongst the other average men who fail to make themselves noticed. Similarly, single women also improve their chances of meeting a partner when they make themselves stand out. Most of the traditional venues that facilitate romantic interaction between single people demand that their inhabitants behave loudly and expressively if they are to succeed in meeting somebody. As such, the need to modify the always-gentle nature of introverts into one that bears a load of charisma presents itself, but can be avoided.

Second, introverted people often allow their own thoughtfulness to get in the way of their romantic endeavors. Many unfortunate introverts report feeling unappreciated when their partners fail to see the value in their thoughtful natures. Not everybody will understand or appreciate a highly thoughtful individual. Your best bet, as an introvert, is to link up with a partner who does. The challenge, then, lies in distinguishing such capable individuals from the rest of the dating pool. Even married couples experience conflict when one partner feels that the other is not coming close to matching their levels of thoughtfulness and consideration.

Third, introverts often struggle in the realm of romance

because they have an intense desire to maintain a level of privacy. Partners of privacy-oriented introverts might feel like the introverted partner has an unwillingness to open up. On the other hand, being private can give you an element of intrigue, as your partners feel enticed to learn about you in small pieces. You might come across like a vault of interesting tidbits that your partner extracts from. However, the fast-paced nature of contemporary society makes being private challenging for romantic relationships; people do not have the patience that they used to. If you make your partner prod you to open up and reveal information about yourself, they may get frustrated and move on to somebody more willing to self-disclose. If somebody is curious about you, do not take that for granted. Your private nature will only charm so long as somebody has a desire to learn about the information that you withhold.

Fourth, introverts often struggle with romantic involvement thanks to the fact that they are more sensitive than the rest of the world. Sensitivity, a trademark characteristic of introverts, makes experiences more meaningful and intense. A sensitive person will allow themselves to wholly experience emotions in ways that other people are incapable of. If a sensitive introvert gets good news, then their whole disposition improves in response. Introverts get great enjoyment out of life's simple pleasures. On the other hand, stressful triggers like loud environments and harsh lighting can make an introvert largely uncomfortable, turning otherwise fun events into challenges. For example, going to a concert, while enjoyable for many, can be unpleasant for introverts because of their sensitivities to jarring bass and flashing lights. Worse yet, not only are introverts sensitive to their environments, they also tend to possess high levels of emotional sensitivity as well. This personality characteristic can lead to misunderstandings when the other person involved in a relationship is unaccommodating of it.

Finally, the mysterious natures of introverts make dating, relationships, and marriage challenging in that mystery creates emotional distance. Not letting other people solve the puzzle that is your personality makes them more likely to feel frustrated and even distrusting. Having a degree of mystery to your personality often creates intrigue and attraction in those who take notice of you. However, as you forge a relationship, your partner will, inevitably, want to know more about you. They will seek to understand what makes you who you are. You cannot keep yourself a mystery forever. You can always maintain a mysterious personality, but you will eventually have to communicate with openness and honesty. Coming to terms with your mysteriousness and using it to your advantage can make this personality trait one of your biggest assets in your dating life if harnessed properly.

Four Types of Introverts

Human introversion takes a number of forms. That number, in fact, is four. Psychologists of recent years are now suggesting that introverts come in multiple varieties: anxious, restrained, thinking, and social. Remembering the acronym ARTS will help you keep these classifications at the forefront of your memory. While the defining traits of these four distinctions make them unique, introverts are united under one common trait: a preference for looking inward.

Anxious introversion takes the form of a tendency to experience anxious thoughts that interfere with daily functions. People who experience anxious introversion prefer solitude over socialization. Their personality characteristics cause self-consciousness and anxiety when in the presence of peers. These individuals have very little confidence in their ability to socialize. Worse yet, in many cases, the anxious feelings cease to dissipate once the individual experiencing them finds solitude. Even when alone, anxious introverts are still prone to the anxious thoughts that distinguish them from other introverts. For example, an anxious introvert may find themselves ruminating over the possibility of a disaster occurring, fretting over an upcoming interview, or sitting in bed and mentally replaying over and over a scenario that they encountered earlier.

Next, restrained introverts, also known as reserved introverts, appear to move at a slower rate cognitively. Restrained introverts tend to take their time and think about what to say before contributing their half of a conversation. Furthermore, they have trouble moving into a working state immediately after waking up. Restrained introverts need time to get moving before they can be expected to concentrate or otherwise function optimally. Like an athlete needs to warm up with light exercise before going into a full-on training routine, a restrained introvert needs to warm up before going into full-force socialization or work.

Moving along, thinking introverts enjoy self-reflection and introspection. What sets them apart from other introverts is their lack of distaste for social situations and events. Thinking introverts, in general, have no problem socializing and meeting people. Rather, their introversion takes the form of deep thought and lengthy reflection. The contents of thinking introverts' thoughts differentiate them from the aforementioned anxious introverts. While anxious introverts tend to focus their thoughts on what might go wrong, thinking introverts tend to dwell on more creative, imaginative thoughts.

Lastly, social introverts fit the profile of the stereotypical introvert, if there is such a thing. They prefer to mingle in very small groups or one-on-one. Large group socialization is undesirable for these people. Sometimes, however, social introverts would rather avoid socializing at all. They are perfectly content staying home and enjoying a book or movie. This is different from anxious introversion in that anxiety, while it may be present, does not influence the preference to avoid large groups. The desire to remain in small groups of close friends does not always imply shyness.

Determining the type of introversion that riddles your personality will help you better understand yourself and your unique needs. Introversion's signs and symptoms extend beyond the preference to avoid large crowds. Labeling someone an introvert can make that person feel misunderstood or oversimplified. Introversion is a complex personality trait that is just as complicated as the lives and personalities of those who exude it.

Common Traits of Introverts

Even though introversion takes four different forms, introverts still share a more or less ubiquitous set of traits that signify an introverted personality. Some are positive; others are found to be a hindrance. In this section, we will examine the personality traits that hint at introversion. If you find yourself experiencing a large percentage of the traits described in this section, then you might be an introvert.

First, being socially active drains introverts. Introverts are unique from extroverted and balanced personalities in that they have to expend a great deal of mental energy on social activity. Extroverts are motivated and energized by socialization; introverts are drained and exhausted by it. Individuals with introverted personalities often leave parties and events a bit earlier than the majority of the crowd because they run out of social energy before most others do. In the absence of a place to escape to, some introverts will zone out after a long period of interpersonal interaction.

Second, introverts are drawn and attracted to extroverts. Introverts often look at extroverts with a sense of admiration at their ability to forget about being serious. Extroverts have a lot to offer introverts in terms of fun and new experiences. The old stereotype that opposites attract holds true in the realm of introversion and extroverted personality types.

Third, introverts experience seemingly nonstop self-talk. The frequency of the inner dialogue or monolog that takes place within your mind can indicate your personality type. If you are constantly interacting with the voice in your head, that might suggest that you are an introvert. Extroverts do not go through the same internal considerations that introverts do. Introverts feel a need to thoroughly think before acting, and the self-talk in their heads helps them make such considerations.

Fourth, environmental surroundings do not affect introverts nearly as much as they do extroverts. Introverts are less motivated by their environments. Studies suggest that extroverts associate strong dopamine rushes with their environments. Introverts simply tend not to process their environment in such a way that makes it rewarding. As a result, introverts have less regard for the effects of their environment. For example, if you have been less than enthused over a venue or location that your companion insisted was amazing, then you are likely introverted.

Fifth, introverts enjoy abstract conversations. While details also intrigue introverts, those details mean nothing to an introvert if he or she cannot fathom how those details contribute to a bigger picture. As such, introverts like to establish an abstract main idea and then support that abstraction with concrete details.

Sixth, introverts like to excel at one thing more than trying their hand at everything. The brain patterns that introverts possess cause them to focus on one concept and engage with all facets of that idea. As a result, introverts tend to develop mastery in specific, concentrated fields and abilities. They enjoy the ability to become an expert in anything but often lack the willingness to engage with unfamiliar experiences or skills.

Seventh, introverts tend to be particularly prone to distraction. While extroverts struggle to contain themselves in the absence of something to do, introverts behave in a directly opposite fashion. When faced with multiple options regarding how to spend time, introverts often shut down to the point of unproductivity. Introverts require a work environment that is free of distracting stimulation. Something as trivial as a light being too bright can distract an introvert's thoughts.

Eighth, introverts excel at public speaking. While mingling with their audience members afterward might be daunting, introverts have a marked ability to hold an audience's attention. You are probably an introvert if you would unquestionably prefer to deliver a speech in front of hundreds than talk to those same people in an interpersonal fashion.

Ninth, seemingly trivial interpersonal interactions like networking and small talk are unappealing to introverts. Introverts like to indulge in deeper topics. As a result, small talk conversations prove cumbersome for those afflicted with introverted personalities. Introverts would rather break past the façade that small talk creates and dive into weightier topics of conversation. Similarly, networking feels incredibly phony to introverts. Networking, the process of conversing with the intent of making career connections, comes across as an attempt to get something out of another individual rather than connect with them.

Tenth, pay attention to your choice of seating when in public. Because introverts dislike being surrounded by people, they often choose to sit at the ends of benches. Similarly, introverts are the first to claim aisle, window, and back row seats in classrooms, public transportation, and theaters.

Eleventh, introversion can affect one's choice of live entertainment. Introverts do not like to shine attention on themselves unless the situation demands it. For example, an introverted performing artist will have no problem putting attention on themselves for the durations of their shows. However, introverts believe that live shows are all about the performers onstage. As such, they go out of their way to avoid attending live events that might involve audience participation.

Twelfth, introverts develop their own working cycles that

alternate between socialization and solitude or work. The fact that introverts need time to recharge from social activity dictates that they maintain a balance of isolation and outgoingness. As such, many introverts will spend weeks at a time focusing on what seems like nothing but their work and individual hobbies, only to suddenly go out socializing several nights a week for a few weeks. The cycles that introverts maintain are developed in attempts to accommodate the unique needs that those with this personality type possess.

Thirteenth, introverts often do not get the credit that they deserve. One strength of introversion is that it gives people the capacity to be incredibly humble. However, that strength can quickly turn into a downside if an introvert does not consciously make their contributions known. Introverts often fail to see the importance in receiving credit for their work, particularly in the workplace. As a result, they often get overshadowed by those who go out of their way to promote their own efforts.

Fourteenth, the phone calls of introverts often go unanswered, even those that come from loved ones. Introverts will not pick up the phone if they are not in a talkative state. When an introvert chooses to place themselves in solitude, they do so because they feel a need to disconnect from human interaction. Ironically, then, your best chances of getting ahold of an introvert over the phone happen when you call them while they are away from home. Introverts screen calls regularly. (On that note, if you call a marked introvert and they do not answer, leave them a message and allow them to return your call at a time that is comfortable to them.)

Fifteenth, introverts tend to enjoy driving alone. Slow traffic will make any sane person lose their mind for a hot second, but open road conditions are an introvert's haven. The combination of solitude, an engaging activity, and their favorite music makes driving alone therapeutic and enjoyable for introverted individuals. When introverts get overwhelmed, long, relaxing drives can put them at ease.

Sixteenth, recent innovations in technology have afforded Westerners the ability to order prepared food over the internet, a feature that introverts love. When faced with the choice, an introvert will choose to order their meal online before they even think about calling the store.

Seventeenth, introverts often sport headphones in public. Headphones signal to the rest of the world that the individual wearing them would prefer to be left alone. An adaptation, the use of headphones as a tool for deterring unwanted conversations has made itself a common practice of introverts. Some even go so far as to wear headphones plugged into nothing; they just want to be left alone.

Eighteenth, introverts are spotted reading in public places. Going out in public is often an uncomfortable experience for individuals with introverted personalities. Books give them a reason to divert their attention away from any potential social activity that might make an unwelcome entrance into their experiences. When faced with an obligation to endure a public outing, introverts sometimes resort to books as their preferred activity while they wait for their companions to finish going about their business.

Lastly, introverts have to contend with the opinions and labels that others assign them. Introverts report being told that they need to come out of their shell or participate more in class, for example. Many introverted individuals also contend with the labels like "quiet," "snobbish," "old soul," and "intense."

You can say with much certainty that you are an introvert if you find that the majority of traits detailed in this section apply to you and your personality. It is entirely possible that an introvert will not display or possess one-hundred percent of these distinguishing traits, but that does not change the fact that these characteristics suggest introversion.

CHAPTER 2

DATING

For our purposes, dating refers to the processes of seeking, meeting, interacting with, and going out on dates with potential romantic partners before committing to a relationship.

Vs. Extroverts

As an introvert, you may have compared yourself to extroverts in the past. Extroverts, after all, seem to get all of the attention, especially from the other single people in proximity. They appear to have the ability to flirt and mingle with ease. As a result, you may have been led to believe that you have to compete in an uphill battle with extroverts for attention from potential mates. Facing such competition from your perspective can get discouraging and overwhelming. Thankfully, you do not have to compete with extroverts for the attention of other single people. You can (and should) embrace your introverted personality and still meet the partner of your dreams.

Especially extroverted people can be attractive because they are comfortable interacting with others because *that is who they are.* If you try to fake extroversion, you will probably come off as incongruent, forced, and weird. Furthermore, if you do establish yourself as an extrovert, you will have to maintain that façade whenever you are in the presence of the people you first behaved in an extroverted fashion towards. Imagine meeting your long-term partner while you faked extroversion, only to have them expect that out of you every time you interact! You can still be introverted and attractive, but this will require that you come to terms with your introversion.

The most attractive introverts (and other people in general) are comfortable with their personalities. Introverted individuals sometimes struggle to find a date because they do not understand the extent of what they can offer somebody else. In other words, such introverts do not feel like they can live up to the standards of potential partners. The most romantically successful introverts embrace their traits and are therefore able to display those traits in such a way that makes them attractive and alluring. So, the first step to achieving dating success as an introvert involves identifying your unique strengths and then figuring out how to make them work for you. In the following section, we will detail the assets that introverts can bring to a romantic relationship.

Strengths of Being an Introvert

First and foremost, introverts are overwhelmingly more self-sufficient than the rest of the population. Whereas extroverts seek external validation, introverts have the uncanny ability to turn inward for confirmation. As such, you have the capacity to lead a relationship, even when your partner doubts your ability to do so. You have the potential to handle relationship conflicts objectively, even if your partner criticizes and blames you for the disagreement. Without a pressing need to gain the approval of others in your way, you can spend more efforts cultivating and managing your relationships.

However, even before entering into a committed relationship, you have a wealth of opportunities to make your quiet personality shine. People who date introverts often praise their respective partners' abilities to remain calm and cool. Because introverts are comfortable without attention and limelight, they are easy to hang out with. Today's rushed, fame-seeking society makes introversion appealing in contrast. If you can convey, subtly, to a potential mate that your chilled out, easy nature can give them a break from the fast-paced world that you live in, then you can give the impression that you are an attractive choice of partners.

Furthermore, introverts are very careful about the words that come out of their mouths. Because introverts spend a fair amount of time considering their words before uttering them, they are less likely to say something regrettable. Many introverts will not speak at all unless they deem it worthwhile to do so. As such, you, as an introvert, are unlikely to say something that will embarrass a partner. Do not make adjustments to this aspect of your personality in attempts to connect with a partner. When conversing with potential mates, you should display your ability to speak with consideration. Hold a conversation, but do not say anything more than you normally would in that situation. Keep your side of the conversation just word-heavy enough to intrigue your potential mate and make them want to know more about you.

In addition, introverts are known for their ability to be incredibly tenacious, a trait that many people desire in a partner. Introverts are able to dedicate themselves to one task and see it through to completion. For example, one introvert reports getting cut from his girlfriend's school's marching band because he did not march according to their standards. He had transferred to that school in order to be nearer to his partner. Rather than lament over the fact that the band leader ignored his musical abilities, this introverted individual took it upon himself to scrutinize and study the marching patterns of the band that he wanted to be a part of. Because the school's band insisted that all members march according to very precise directions, many people failed to make it past the first round of tryouts. However, our hero in this story was able to meticulously learn and eventually memorize the band's preferred marching patterns. As a result, he was brought into the band after he tried out again the next year. Similarly, you have the capacity to manage relationships with the same resolve. You can and are willing to examine weak points in your relationships and strengthen them. If you are unsure of how to do so, you will have no trouble researching the relationship problem and its solutions. After all, the fact that you picked up this book is already a testament to your studious tenacity.

Next, the intellectually stimulating nature of introverts makes them attractive choices of romantic partners. Introverts dislike small talk because they prefer to dive into more stimulating topics of conversation. This part of their personality can repel those who expect a "normal" conversation with potential mates; however, introverts have a lot to offer in terms of intellectual stimulation. Because introverts spend a lot of time in states of self-reflection, they develop the capacity to deeply explore ideas. Demonstrate this capacity to a potential mate by diving deep into a conversation *about them*. When you are able to convey that you understand another person on a deeper level, or that you are at least able to, you become more attractive in their eyes. Nobody wants a partner who does not "get" them. Your introversion can be your best asset when it comes to demonstrating your natural strengths, including the ability to explore, grasp, and understand the deeper, more subtle aspects of other people. As an added bonus, your potential partners will feel like they do not have to "come clean" if you can communicate that you already have an idea of how they think and act. Make use of your introverted analytical skills and apply them to the lives of the people with whom you converse.

Also, introverts are excellent listeners. Most introverts listen way more than they speak, which often earns them the label of "quiet." However, your listening capabilities are probably some of your best assets when it comes to dating, relationships, and marriage. The extroverts of the world are usually preoccupied with their own lives and obligations, and rightfully so. However, active listening, the process of listening to another person with the intent to understand and empathize, is an incredibly attractive practice. When partners actively listen to one another, the connection between them strengthens. Listen not just to reply, but to engage as well.

Moreover, introverts possess a great capacity for divergent thinking. In other words, they are creative. The act of existing in a state of solitude for extended periods of time breeds creativity. While in solitude, humans are more likely and abler to focus deeply, think outside of the box, and act creatively. Creativity is an attractive trait. Consider the fact that our tribal ancestors contended with problems that they had never heard of with no way of researching how to deal with such a problem. For example, a migrating herd of predatory cats might have made their way into a village for the first time, leaving that tribal neighborhood's inhabitants to figure out a way to deal with the foreign non-human invaders. Tribespeople who could not improvise a defense against aggressive sabretooth tigers would die, while those who successfully survived unheard of problems passed down their creative genes. As such, creativity has evolutionary survival implications and, therefore, is an attractive trait.

Moving on, introverts are blessed with independent natures. If you can subtly demonstrate your capacity for independence to a potential mate, you stand to make yourself more attractive. While having a partner present when you need support is wonderful, nobody wants a partner who is wholly dependent on them. In addition, your independent nature suggests to potential partners that you can at least take care of yourself, which hints that you just might be able to care for a partner when they need you the most. You can demonstrate the resolve and extent of your independent nature by telling a story about a time when you had to fend for yourself while overcoming adversity. For example, I like to bring up how I took on a second job while attending college full time to help pay my hospital bills after I dislocated my elbow four years into my sports entertainment career, which I worked very hard to establish. You get the point.

Lastly, introverts have an amazing tendency to take care of their own well-beings. You might not want to make yourself stand out amongst a crowd, but you can still go out of your way to rise above the competition in terms of cleanliness and overall health and appearance. Introverts know the value of maintaining a healthy body. Solitude helps people develop a meticulous self-care routine. For example, introverts are often seen wearing nice clothing while well-groomed. They are like less noticeable models. When you go out of your way to take care of yourself, potential mates will notice. Again, the ability to care for yourself implies an ability to care for a partner when they need you. In contrast, if you fail to maintain certain grooming and hygiene standards, otherwise potential partners will be repelled. If you cannot care for yourself, how can anyone expect you to care for them when they need you to? Demonstrate your uncanny ability to take care of yourself; put effort towards hygiene, grooming, and dressing well.

In sum, you can harness your introverted qualities and tendencies in such a way that promotes your most attractive offerings. Namely, your self-sufficiency, calm composure, careful manner of speaking, tenacity, intellectual stimulation capabilities, active listening skills, creativity, independent nature, and self-care abilities can make you a catch in the eyes of potential mates. Next, we will explore how you can go about seeking and meeting a partner with those considerations in mind.

Dating Tips for Introverts

Dating is hard enough without introvert tendencies tripping you up along the way. This section is designed to help introverts achieve success in their dating lives through practical, applicable tips that are often situation-specific.

First, parties are a great place to meet your next fling. However, introverts go about parties differently than the rest of the population does. While extroverted partygoers see parties as opportunities to socialize with new people and make a great number of new connections, introverts prefer to enjoy the company of the people that they already know. As a whole, the introverted population does not enjoy parties any more or less than the extroverts do; they just enjoy them differently. As such, introverts should attend parties without comparing their social activity to extroverts because to do so would be a losing battle against one's own insecurities.

Instead, introverts must accept that they are, in fact, introverted and plan to party accordingly. To illustrate, introverts feel better about parties when they plan to attend, but only for a small amount of time. Instead of partying all night until the booze is gone, consider only mingling for two hours or so with the intention of moving your social activity elsewhere with a smaller group. For example, if you plan on attending a party with friends, make plans with them ahead of time to leave the gathering to go out to eat at a certain time in the evening. Then, if you meet a potential mate at the party, you can invite that person to join you and your friends in a small-group context that you are more comfortable in.

Second, consider online dating. Introverts tend to be more proficient with written communication than oral, face-to-face communication. Therefore, online dating makes an optimal choice of partner-finding media. Capitalize on your written communication skills and seek partners digitally. In addition, your online mate-meeting endeavors are not limited to dating platforms. You can also meet people on forums, message boards, and social media platforms. Alex Plank, the founder of wrongplanet.net, a popular online forum for discussing autism and autism-related issues, reports that many married couples originally met on his website. While you may not be immediately seeking a spouse, this anecdote serves as evidence of the fact that online communication can facilitate romantic relationships.

Third, open yourself up to casual conversation. It is well-established at this point that introverts at least dislike small talk. However, that is not a reason to dismiss its potential to develop into something more. Many people meet their spouse during chance conversations that they never expect to turn into anything beyond a friendly, one-off interaction.

Fourth, try to focus your attention away from yourself. This can be difficult for anyone, especially those who are accustomed to spending time engaged in self-reflection. However, when you go about your dating life overly focused on yourself, you distract yourself from the task at hand: finding out if the person in your presence might be worth building a future with. So, the next time you find yourself at a social gathering, pick out one person in the room and make a point to find out more about them. You already know a lot about yourself; take yourself out of your mental spotlight. Think "there you are" instead of "look at me."

Fifth, place yourself in positions to meet people in environments that you find comfortable. Many introverts hate the prospect of enduring crowded clubs and bars in exchange for the chance to talk to somebody who might or might not be worth knowing. Thankfully, more comfortable alternatives to dating exist. Consider investing time in a hobby that facilitates interpersonal interaction. For example, you might get involved with art classes, volunteer opportunities, or team sports and athletic endeavors. These activities give you the chance to meet people organically and expand your social network so that you might meet a partner without subjecting yourself to uncomfortable environments and situations.

To summarize, finding and meeting a date does not have to be a puzzle for introverts. Simple, concrete adjustments to your approach can make the difference between a successful outing and a return home without a date lined up. So, to make the most of your social opportunities, plan your partying in an accommodating fashion, try your hand at meeting others online, embrace small talk, shine attention completely away from yourself, and put yourself in situations that will help you meet people in ways that work for you.

Your Dating Life

You cannot avoid going on dates. Dating is the primary means by which relationships form. Your introverted personality might make you dread the idea of spending extended time with another person, but you definitely have to do it if you want to meet a romantic partner. Thankfully, unless you live in a country that oppresses the rights of certain genders and ethnic groups, you have the right to determine your own boundaries in this process. You are not obligated to choose any one course of action throughout your dating endeavors. For example, if you find that going on more than one date in a two-week period is too draining, you can limit the number of dates that you agree to go on.

On that note, you must take care to avoid experiencing dating related FOMO. Also known as fear of missing out, FOMO happens to people when they feel left out or left behind with regards to the activities of their peer groups. So, you might experience FOMO if you see one or more of your friends going out on multiple dates in one weekend, posting couples pictures on social media, and so on. Understand that you and the members of your social circles and networks have unique, different personalities. What might be suitable for one person's dating life could be counterproductive for another's. If you have an introverted personality, you might find yourself overwhelmed if you agree to go on more dates than you can handle, especially if interpersonal interaction has the potential to wipe you of your mental energy. As such, adhere to a dating calendar that works for you and your personality.

Along those same lines, if you feel like rescheduling a date would improve your chances of making a good impression when the date does happen, then do that. You might find yourself unable to muster up the energy and shine required to engage with another individual. Worse yet, your date is scheduled to take place in seven hours. If a situation like this ever happens to you, your best bet is to call your date and inform them that you wish to reschedule. You do not have to offer a drawn-out explanation or detailed reason, but you should make it clear that you do want to go on the date, only at a later time. Ignore any FOMO and take care of your own needs first.

Finding Fellow Introverts

Relationships between introverts tend to work because both parties understand the personality traits of one another to a large degree. Introverted couples can get away with not needing to compromise their personalities in order to accommodate the needs of one another. As such, your most fulfilling relationship might bloom out of a date with a fellow introvert.

If you happen to find yourself single at a party, then you could very well meet your next partner there! When mingling at a party, try seeking out fellow introverts. Introverts are easy to spot; people with introverted personalities display a number of recognizable behaviors at parties. Namely, they remain along perimeters and exclude themselves from large groups. Much like their extroverted counterparts, introverts do enjoy and benefit from socializing and mingling. However, they go about those activities differently than extroverts do. While extroverts tend to congregate in large, centrally located groups at parties, introverts tend to huddle up in small groups or pairs, usually near the edges of rooms. Additionally, introverted party attendees might be seen entertaining themselves with activities that do not involve interacting with other people, such as playing with a pet, grazing the snack table, or watching any live musicians that might be performing. If you spot a fellow introvert at a party, strike up a conversation with them. If your introvert-spotting abilities are to be trusted, your new acquaintance will probably be happy to fast-forward through small talk and delve into more meaningful subjects.

In addendum, many introverts enjoy hosting parties and would prefer to do so instead of attending another person's. Hosting has a wealth of benefits that introverts desire, including the ability to determine the party's hours, attendees, and environment. Hosts have the capacity to manipulate parties to a degree so that they feel comfortable in what would otherwise seem like an overwhelming scenario. Hosting allows introverts the opportunity to socialize in a party atmosphere while reducing the risk of experiencing uncomfortable uncertainties and variables. In addition, hosts have a valid reason to escape conversations if they feel the need to; their hosting obligations can pull them away from an interaction at a moment's notice. So, you might have success meeting a fellow introvert if you take it upon yourself to get to know the host. In addition, hosting your own party or parties will afford you opportunities to meet people in a controlled environment of your liking. Consider hosting a social gathering if you have the means to do so. Encourage your friends to invite their friends. If you have trouble making a sufficient guest list, consider publicizing your party on social gathering platforms like Meetup and Eventbrite.

Thankfully, your chances of encountering fellow introverts are great in environments that do not contain large crowds or expectations of social interaction. For example, many introverts, single ones included, enjoy spending time in nature. The great outdoors offers introverts the opportunity to get away from overwhelming crowds of people and explore the world at their own leisure. Consider joining a club that facilitates nature exploration endeavors like hikes and trail walks. Because of the nature-loving tendencies of introverts, many such organizations are overflowing with introverted personality types. Outdoor clubs facilitate and encourage interaction between members, eliminating or at least reducing the awkwardness that comes with approaching strangers outside of social gatherings. Even if nature is not necessarily your thing, joining such a club will improve your chances of meeting a fellow introvert and give you opportunities to explore environments you may have never thought to visit on your own.

Seeing Through Pseudo-Extroverts

Many well-meaning introverts successfully disguise themselves as extroverts. They do so because they have a desire to possess the outgoing nature of extroverts, so they effectively mimic extroverted personality traits. A seemingly extroverted person might, in fact, be an introvert disguised as the opposite personality type. When an introvert takes on a number of extroverted behaviors, they do so because they have an intense desire to experience the same social experiences that extroverts enjoy. As such, pseudo-extroverts are usually, on the surface, open to interactions with many individuals. As an introvert, you have a great chance of striking up a conversation and deeply connecting with a pseudo-introvert. Recognizing and knowing the telltale signs of pseudo-extroverts will help your chances of meeting them.

First, pseudo-extroverts tend to zone out, especially in the midst of heavy social interaction. Introverts, as you know by now, tend to get overwhelmed by populated social situations. Pseudo-extroverts cope with this tendency by zoning out. Spacing out affords them the opportunity to block out external stimuli and gather their bearings. Somebody who alternates between periods of intense socializing and silent daydreaming is likely a pseudo-extrovert.

Second, introverts in disguise tend to leave parties earlier than the rest of the attendees. Pseudo-extroverts like to mingle at parties before the events go into full swing. They get a sudden uncomfortableness to when party attendees get too involved for their preferences. If you notice somebody who regularly leaves a party early, despite seeming to have a great time socializing, consider approaching them as if they were a pseudo-extrovert.

Third, these disguised personalities will often be found remaining close to a small number of select individuals throughout the course of the event. Introverts at heart, pseudo-extroverts cannot avoid some of their natural tendencies, including the desire to stay in the company of familiar individuals.

Such individuals also tend to demonstrate a special fascination with the artwork, literature, and unique décor found at the party's environment. They tend to give extra attention to pets and prefer to help out with less social tasks like disk jockeying, cleaning, and preparing food. If you spot an attractive pseudo-extrovert at a social gathering, approach them! They have the learned ability to hold a social interaction and simultaneously connect with fellow introverts in ways that they cannot with extroverts.

Avoid Alcohol

Alcohol, often hailed in the dating world as a "social lubricant," can have disastrous effects for introverts in particular. Most people are aware of alcohol's ability to turn anyone, introverted or not, into an obnoxious nuisance. However, introverts face another risk when they drink during the dating process: losing the ability to determine if the other person is right for them.

As an introvert, you probably take great care to only let the most real, most thoughtful people into your life. Alcohol impairs your ability to judge the characters of others. As such, it is to be avoided if you intend to exercise a degree of selectivity when determining the potential of a future with your date. As an introvert, you likely go through dating with much more selectivity than your extroverted peers.

Furthermore, alcohol is often abused as a crutch. If you

depend on alcohol to loosen you up to the point of sociability, you are teaching yourself to depend on a foreign substance. And, as you probably already know, dependence is an early point on the path to addiction.

So, your best bet as an introvert is to avoid consuming alcohol, especially on your first date with somebody. Opt for caffeinated non-alcoholic beverages instead. They will still promote a talkative nature, but will not impede on your ability to effectively judge the character of your date. After all, you just might end up spending the rest of your life with this person. Allow yourself to get to know your date so that you do not end up choosing the wrong lifelong partner later.

CHAPTER 3

RELATIONSHIPS

The relationship stage, defined for our purposes as the period of courtship that takes place between dating and marriage, requires active management and a willingness to compromise. As an introvert, you will have to contend with your unique skills and challenges that comprise your personality. Navigating a relationship as an introvert has its upsides as well as its disadvantages.

Advantages of Introversion in Relationships

As an introvert, you can offer partners certain advantages that extroverts cannot. Introverts usually thrive in relationships that are established beyond the dating phase. In other words, committed, exclusive one-on-one romantic relationships are an introvert's specialty. Connecting deeply with one special individual makes itself much easier for introverts than meeting and interacting with relative strangers. As such, introverts interested in romantic relationships should understand the strengths that they bring to committed relationships.

First, introverts can provide their partners with a relaxing space. Introverts, usually quiet and reserved in nature, handle relationships with a cool demeanor. Extroverted partners of introverts report enjoying the calming influence that their partners have on them.

Second, introverts are comfortable letting their respective partners have the spotlight. This is especially beneficial for introverts in relationships with extroverted partners. Introverts tend not to get jealous when their respective partners get attention from others who might even be interested in them. Most introverts are confident enough in their own worth to avoid worrying about their partner taking center stage and leaving them in the dark at times. In fact, some introverts even prefer such an arrangement, living vicariously through their respective partners' experiences. As such, introverts possess the uncanny ability to confidently sit back while their respective partners enjoy the limelight.

Third, most introverts are great at learning from their own mistakes and taking steps to avoid committing those same errors in the future. Because introverts value peace and quiet, they develop an incredible capacity to reflect on and come to terms with their own shortcomings. For example, if an introvert wrongfully says something hurtful to their partner out of anger and spite, they are usually quick to realize their mistake and admit to it. The amount of self-reflection that introverts do contributes to this strength of theirs. Introverts place value on traits like integrity and thoughtfulness.The prospect of a romantic partner who can easily admit when they are wrong appeals to the vast majority of people.

Similarly, introverts possess the strength of care. They excel at empathizing with and understanding the needs and emotions of others. This trait manifests itself in an ability to deeply connect with a partner. Awareness of your partner's thoughts and feelings will give you the perspective needed to understand them more completely.

As a result of their careful nature, introverts also have a strong ability to build great levels of rapport with romantic partners. Introverts are less interested in trivial topics of discussion like current events and weather; they prefer to get involved in more "real" conversations. Rapport strengthens relationships. Thankfully, introverts excel in that area, thanks in no small part to their patient natures. Introverts, in their desire to get into deep conversation, are usually the ones who help make the sometimes uncomfortable transition to heavier topics of conversation that build strong rapport. For example, introverts typically take it upon themselves to move into touchy topics of conversation like morals, sexuality, and religious allegiances. While sensitive, the attitudes that partners have on these subjects have the potential to make or break a relationship. Moreover, they will eventually have to arise as a romantic relationship progresses. Thankfully, introverts know just how to bring up these topics without putting undue pressure on the situation.

Finally, committed romantic relationships are great for introverts in that honesty takes a front seat. Crucial to the health of any relationship, honesty is an introvert's strong suit. Introverts despise the drama and conflict that dishonesty has the potential to cause. As a result, introverts tend to be more honest with their partners than their extroverted counterparts are. Introverts do not enjoy hiding who they are.

As an introvert, you have a lot that you can bring to a romantic relationship. Recognizing your strengths and abilities is crucial to understanding how you contribute to such an arrangement. Remember, introverts provide partners with a calm nature, lack of jealousy, error correction capabilities, care, rapport, and honesty.

Introvert-Introvert Relationships

Introvert-introvert relationships, or romantic arrangements

between pairs of introverts, often work better than do relationships between individuals of varying personality types. The previous chapter provided suggestions for finding and meeting another introvert; this section will detail the potential benefits that such relationships provide in addition to suggestions for managing such a relationship.

The primary upside of dating another introvert comes in the form of an intuitive understanding between the two of you. Introverts have an easier time making their needs known to other introverts. Nonverbal communication between introverts is usually less ambiguous than nonverbal communication between, say, and introvert and an extrovert.

First, be okay with it if your partner wants to stay at home while you go out. There will inevitably be times where you have a disagreement regarding whether to stay home or leave the house. When each person can do their own thing without guilt or obligation, introvert-introvert relationships flourish. Similarly, let your partner go out and enjoy a night out while you stay at home if you want to stay in. However, on the occasion that the both of you want to either go out or stay in together, enjoy yourselves.

Second, share uncomfortable responsibilities evenly. As introverts, you and your introverted partner probably have reservations about performing tasks like talking to customer service representatives. When you take turns handling such unfavorable obligations, you maintain a sense of fairness and equality in the relationship. On the other hand, when one partner gets stuck with all of the undesirable responsibilities, resentments often arise. Ensure that your relationship is fair and balanced by evenly dividing up your least favorite tasks. Other less-than-desirable tasks to be divided up might include questioning a salesperson, answering the door for delivery persons, and calling to make a payment or place an order by phone.

Third, make going out fun. Introverts often struggle to convince themselves to leave the house. However, if you can make your regular couple outings more enjoyable, then your relationship will benefit from the fun that you have outside of your home. For example, if you have to go to a networking event, plan a date at your favorite restaurant with your partner that takes place shortly after the end of your obligatory gathering. Or, if you want to go out while your partner insists on staying in, you might try bribing them to leave the house with the promise of a fun experience that they can only have if they go out with you. For example, you might promise to let your partner pick out the movies for your next three at-home movie night dates if they muster up the courage to accompany you to a party. Incentivizing yourselves to exit your comfort zones will help you and your partner handle your out-of-the-house obligations with optimism.

Fourth, pledge to keep all communication honest, direct, and holistic. There may be times in an introvert-introvert relationship where one partner has a hard time interpreting the disposition of the other. Because external triggers can lead to drastic changes in the attitudes of introverts, you might find yourself wondering if your introverted partner's distant attitude is a result of your behavior, for example. If you find yourself in such a situation, do not be afraid to ask your partner about the cause of their slightly off disposition. Of course, you will want to find out whether your partner is upset with you or if they are just displaying their introverted tendencies. Promise to each other to always ask about such uncertainties and that you will not get offended at such questions

Do Not Ignore Your Friends

When a relationship is strong, fresh, and smooth, the partners involved do make efforts to spend as much time with each other as possible, either in person or through digitally mediated communication platforms. Some new parties to a relationship make the mistake of neglecting relationships with friends and family so that they can put more effort into their committed relationships.

However, when and if the romantic relationship comes to an end, the parties involved will benefit from having a strong support system. In other words, after a breakup, humans are best off when their friends are there for them. As such, it is important to maintain somewhat of a relationship with your friends, even when your partner draws all of your attention.

Because introverts tend to keep a small, tightly bonded circle of friends, their needs to maintain those friendships throughout the course of a relationship are doubly important. You do not have to call your friends every day, but a simple text message every so often will let them know that you still think about and value them as friends.

Your close friends do not want to lose you to a new partner, but they should also not demand that you maintain the same commitment to them that you did pre-relationship. Real friends will understand that you have a new partner and, as such, will have reasonably less time for them. However, that is not to suggest that you have permission to wholly ignore your other real-world connections in favor of one sexy individual. Think about who will be there for you if your relationship ends; cherish those people.

Take Care of Your Own Needs

Successful relationships are the ones in which both parties establish their own boundaries, needs, and wants while respecting one another's. The responsibility to communicate the needs of your introverted personality to your partner lies in your hands. Specifically, introverts often require time in solitude. Make it clear to your partner that you need regular alone time, taking care to explain your reasoning. Inform your partner that, as an introvert, you regularly need time to yourself. Articulate that your desire for solo time has nothing to do with a desire to get away from your partner, but rather, stems from a need to recharge in solitude. Reinforce this point until your partner grasps the idea that you would need time away from anybody, not just them specifically. In the event that your romantic partner is extroverted, the requirement for alone time becomes more pressing than it would in an introvert-introvert arrangement.

On the other hand, if you enjoy a romantic relationship with a fellow introvert, then your need for time apart may dissipate or decline. Because introverts understand that silence between them does not suggest distance, they can maintain relationships in which they indulge in alone time while in the presence of one another. For example, many introverted couples enjoy reading or otherwise just hanging out in the same room while they remain largely silent or non-interactive. In any case, determining, communicating, and negotiating your introverted needs is crucial to the long-term success of your romantic relationships.

CHAPTER 4

MARRIAGE

Marriages are unique contractual agreements in that they do not guarantee any sort of outcome. Business contracts and other legally binding agreements guarantee that all parties involved in the negotiations end up with something as soon as the contract takes effect. For example, corporate businesspeople might sign a contract in which one party trades services for money and equity from the other. On the other hand, a marriage contract does not guarantee anything to either party, aside from a few tax and insurance benefits. The unpredictable world of marriage provides great fulfillment to those who navigate it effectively.

Coping with Sleeping Patterns

Introverts, as a whole, possess different sleeping needs than the rest of the population. As a married person, you will be living with another human being. Moving in with a new spouse is akin to getting a new roommate. As such, you and your spouse will have to contend with and accommodate the biological needs of one another. Sleeping arrangements are no exception. This section is designed to help introverts understand and articulate sleeping tendencies that might need to be negotiated as part of a marriage.

In general, introverts require and desire more sleep than their extroverted counterparts. While most extroverts would forgo sleep entirely if they could, introverts welcome the break from full consciousness. Sleep, according to introverts, provides a chance to refresh the mind and escape from the hectic environments that plague their waking daylight hours. As such, you will need to communicate your need for sleep to your partner. Your partner should understand that your elevated sleep requirements do not suggest laziness or other shortcomings on your part; rather, the need to get extra sleep is just a result of your ingrained personality type.

Additionally, introverts find sleep therapeutic. Dreams provide introspective individuals with a chance to explore the depths of their unconscious psyche. Understanding the self is often a relieving experience, especially for those with introverted personality types.

Similarly, introverts tend to stay up and sleep in later than do their extroverted counterparts. The late hours of the day provide a scenario in which introverts thrive: a quiet, slow-paced environment that allows time for distraction-free reflection. Because introverts value introspection, nighttime environments often invigorate their minds. While other people snore, introverts enjoy contemplating and reflecting on past experiences, future considerations, and random assortments of other ponderings. In the night, introverts often get highly engaged with their internal monologs because of the fact that the demands that contemporary working hours place on society do not afford them that opportunity when the sun is out.

You will need to communicate to your spouse that your personality comes equipped with unique sleeping habits that might seem strange or abnormal to regular extroverts. Negotiating sleeping arrangements in your marriage will help you and your spouse get the rest that each of you needs without interfering with the needs of others. If needed, you might have to allow a spouse who goes to sleep early to enjoy a quiet bedroom while you stay awake in another area of the house. While your spouse should respect your natural sleeping habits, you must also respect and accommodate theirs. Do not make them feel guilty for wanting to get some sleep when you would rather they stay up and hang out. Similarly, if you are accommodating of your spouse's sleeping habits, then you can expect them to refrain from prodding you to wake up before you are ready. Sleep, according to Abraham Maslow, is a basic human need that must be met before a relationship can thrive. Spouses that go through their marriage in a constant state of tiredness will, when all other variables are equal, not enjoy the same quality of marriage as will a well-rested couple.

Prioritize Your Roles

Relationships of all types, social, business, and otherwise, dictate that the parties involved maintain their own roles. For example, a business relationship between two individuals might place one person in the role of supervisor while the other takes on the role of a subordinate. Similarly, you likely have several social and professional roles that you play, including but not limited to romantic partner, parent, student, and friend. As such, it is important that you prioritize your roles so that you afford each of them an appropriate portion of your limited time.

For example, if you are a parent, it would be ill-advised to neglect your young kids in favor of going on a date with a new romantic partner. As such, determining how much priority you place on each of your roles will help determine the overall quality of your life.

As an introvert, you probably value your deepest friendships dearly. So, you might not be so high on the idea of putting them on the back burner to accommodate a new romantic partner. There is no one-size-fits-all prescription for prioritizing the roles that one plays in life. Instead, individuals must determine how they want to run their own lives. This can be a tricky process, as spending an abundance of time in one role might cause others to go neglected.

Thankfully, as an introvert, you likely prefer to maintain a small number of deep relationships over a large number of surface-level ones. This means that your risk of stretching your attention too thin runs lower than the risk levels that your extroverted counterparts face. However, you may have to inform your partner that your children will take priority over them, for example. In any case, take the time to consider how much time and effort you can appropriately dedicate to each of your roles in life. Make adjustments as needed.

Select Carefully

Assuming that you intend to maintain a long-term monogamous relationship, you, as an introvert, need to be more selective than extroverts. Because of your capacity to develop incredibly deep, meaningful rapport, you and your spouse will likely end up revealing a lot about yourselves to one another if your marriage lasts for a while. As such, you will likely end up seeing many sides of your partner and their character that an extroverted person never would. Therefore, many dating columnists advise introverts to exercise an added degree of selectivity when choosing long-term romantic partners.

Do not rush into a committed meaningful relationship with the first person who takes an interest in you. You will need to get a deep understanding of their character and personality before you can commit to that person. Your introversion is a gift and a curse in that you bring out deeply hidden aspects of other people's personalities. With regards to romantic relationships, that means that you will need to be extremely selective if you are to enjoy a successful lifelong commitment with another human being. Do not, however, let the guise of selectivity deter you from pursuing contact with somebody that you think you might have a future with.

You should be sure beyond a shadow of a doubt that your romantic partner is "the one" before you commit to marrying them. The intuition capabilities that your introverted personality has likely blessed you with will assist you in your selectivity.

Encourage Your Spouse to Socialize Elsewhere

I am not suggesting that you tell your partner to leave you

alone. Rather, your spouse should understand that they are encouraged to maintain nonromantic relationships outside of the marriage. Encourage your spouse to maintain an active social life that they can enjoy either with or without you. This will allow your spouse the opportunity to have fun while they simultaneously cater to your introverted personality.

As an added benefit, spouses of introverts who keep a social circle outside of the marriage tend to have more fulfilling marriages. When a married person gets the chance to socialize with friends and acquaintances, they are less likely to depend on their spouse for all of their socialization needs. So, a socially active spouse will let you enjoy nights to yourself and keep themselves socially fulfilled at the same time. Never discourage your spouse from going out with their friends, especially when you would rather spend time in solitude. Of course, if you worry about your spouse participating in inappropriate extramarital activities on nights when they let you be alone, then that is a separate issue that your introverted personality is not responsible for.

If your spouse's friends do not have a lot of spare time for socializing with them, encourage more formal social arrangements for them. For example, suggest that they join a club, poker league, or amateur sports team. Any healthy social activity that will keep your spouse entertained while you get your much-needed solitude will help your marriage thrive.

Furthermore, if absence causes the heart to become fonder, then your scheduled solitude will make it that much sweeter when your spouse returns from his or her nights out. If your spouse has an extroverted personality, they will return from their social outings energized and happy to see you while you get to feel refreshed and relaxed from your time alone. Either way, keeping your spouse busy while they afford you solitude will help keep the marriage happy.

Along those same lines, if one spouse wants to go out to an event that you were both invited to as a couple, it is perfectly okay for the other to stay behind. Taking your spouse along with you when they prefer not to come along will cause them to resent you, and vice versa. Let each spouse maintain their autonomy and choose how they spend their free time, so long as they do not violate any of the marriage's expectations along the way.

Find Solitude in Public

It is no secret by now that introverts tend to thrive off of solitude. However, solitude is not limited to time spent alone in the privacy of your own home. Rather, you can find a solitude of sorts out in public. For example, some introverts report feeling refreshed after browsing their local shopping mall with a pair of headphones on. In addition, taking a walk or jog at an outdoor park can provide introverts with the break that they need. It is unfair to expect your spouse to let you have your shared home to yourself every time you need a moment to yourself. As such, you may have to adapt to cohabitation by finding solitude outside of the home. You should not neglect your introverted needs in order to appease a partner. However, you may have to cater to them in innovative ways that you did not consider during your time living without a partner.

Always be Communicating

Communication is an essential component to any healthy relationship, romantic or otherwise. However, without effective communication, a marriage is bound to fail. You and your spouse are unique individuals with unique needs. Communicating the needs that relate to your introverted personality might prove difficult, especially if your spouse does not display many introverted tendencies. Expect that it might take time for a spouse to grasp your introversion and its implications.

Along those same lines, you cannot expect your spouse to accommodate your personality if you fail to adjust to theirs. For example, if you marry an extrovert, understand that they may very well have an intense need to be social. If that is the case, allow them to enjoy nights on the town with large groups of people. Do not feel obligated to come along on your spouse's social outings, but do not try to prevent them from enjoying some harmless socialization with their friends. If your spouse tries to pressure you into going out and the prospect of doing so makes you uncomfortable, communicate with them and inform them of your reservations about large groups of people.

Similarly, do not allow an extroverted spouse pressure you into accompanying them to a social event when you would much rather enjoy some quiet time. It is your responsibility to articulate your need for solitude. A spouse who respects your personality will understand and let you choose how you spend your free time.

So, how do you effectively articulate your introverted needs to your spouse? More importantly, how do you negotiate those needs with the socialization needs of your spouse? You have to be concise, specific, and concrete. You cannot get away with mentioning that you "sometimes need to be alone" and expect that off-handed comment to suffice. What frequency does "sometimes" imply? When you say you need to be "alone," do you need your spouse to just go to another room for fifteen minutes, or do you require hours of solitude without any other people in your vicinity?

Next, come up with a strategy for meeting your needs. You might agree that your spouse will give you the apartment to yourself at least one night a week, for example. Furthermore, you could come to an agreement that allows you to isolate yourself from your spouse for up to two hours without question. Your unique needs will determine the strategies that you craft for going about meeting them.

If seemingly unresolvable communication issues plague the success of your marriage, consider seeking professional couples' therapy.

Take Turns Leading

If you and your spouse's personalities are aligned in such a way that interferes with agreements about your social lives, consider taking turns deciding how to go about social events. For example, your extroverted spouse might insist that you go out and interact with friends as a couple while you prefer to stay at home and enjoy the company of one another. In cases such as this one, switching off the spouse responsible for determining social activity can prove beneficial. Doing so will allow each spouse to experience the world of their partner.

In addition, introducing your spouse to social activities that they are not used to is a great way to help the two of you understand one another. Seeing how your partner likes to socialize will give you great insight into why they are the way that they are.

So, when date night rolls around, determine whose turn it is to pick the date's activity. The spouse in charge of this will get to pick the activity that the two of you partake in for the evening. For example, your spouse might take you to a casino one weekend, leaving you free to choose a movie night at home the next.

CONCLUSION

Thank you for reaching the ending of *The Quiet Cupid: An Introvert's Guide to Love, Marriage, and Relationships*. I sincerely hope that you enjoyed it and found it to be a valuable tool in achieving your love, marriage, and relationship goals, whatever those might be.

The next step is to consciously apply the knowledge offered in the pages of this book to your personal life. Theories and information will only take you so far; the responsibility to make use of your newly acquired perspectives is solely yours. In this book, we discussed introversion and its implications in dating, relationships, and marriages.

If you like to hear about my other projects, please visit the address below.

http://clika.pe/l/13430/56723/

Finally, if you found this book useful in any way, a review on

Amazon is always appreciated! I can only improve this material if you let me know what I'm doing wrong. Think of it as "paying it forward" for the next reader, by letting them know your experience.